Bearded Dragons,

Basic Beardie Care

Bearded Dragons,
Basic Beardie Care

Sheryl Wilson,
Christopher Wilson,
and Nicholas Wilson

Samati Press,
Sacramento, Clifornia

ISBN 978-1-949125-12-2 (Print Version)
ISBN 978-1-949125-13-9 (Digital versions)
Library of Congress Control Number: 2020910553

Edited by Sharon S Darrow

Publisher: Samati Press
Sacramento, California

Manufactured in the United States of America

Contents

Chapter One
Are Bearded Dragons Good Pets?

Yes! Bearded Dragons are great pets—the perfect choice for first-time reptile owners—which is why they're the most popular reptile pets in the country. They're alert, awake during the daytime, require easy care compared to other reptiles, and enjoy interacting with their humans. They have their own individual personalities and bond with their people, but are also quite self-sufficient without needing lots of attention. Many Beardies enjoy being held, and will run to the door of their cage wanting to get out when their person comes near. Good training and socialization is the key to this kind of interaction.

Beardies can be the answer for people who thought they couldn't have pets. A "no pet" clause in a lease can be devastating, but they seldom prohibit caged pets. That means your Beardie can be the perfect answer. Bearded

Dragons can also be the answer for people with pet allergies. No fur means no fur dander, so an allergy doesn't have to mean a household without a beloved pet.

Bearded Dragons, like other pets, need proper socialization to build a great relationship with its humans. One way to acclimate a new Beardie is to place a small item of clothing that has been worn by the owner into the cage for the first couple of weeks. This will permit them to get used to the scent and connect it to the person feeding and handling them. Handling them a lot is an important part of socialization. Your new Beardie might be testy at first, puffing its beard and even opening its mouth if you put your hand close. It's nervous about the new surroundings, and may not have had a lot of interaction with humans at his previous home. Take your time, go slow, but handle it a lot to tame it down.

Children are often fascinated by reptiles, and a Bearded Dragon can be an ideal first reptile pet. It's easy for children to learn how to care for Beardies, but they should always be supervised by adults.

Chapter Two
How Long do Bearded Dragons Live?

Captive-bred Beardies can live for twelve to fifteen years, with proper husbandry. The key is the same for people—proper environment, good nutrition, health care, and genetics. The owner controls everything except the genetics, which is why learning where your Bearded Dragon came from can make a big difference.

Just in case you're wondering, almost all the Beardies you might consider for a pet will be captive bred. Bearded Dragons were brought to this country from Australia, and became popular pets right away. Australia has strict laws prohibiting exportation of Beardies and other native animals, so wild born Bearded Dragons are not available. The term "Normal" Bearded Dragons refer to ones that most favor the Australian natives, which range from gray to a sandy brown. The fancy colors—bright yellow, orange, red, pale gray—and striking patterns were developed in captive-bred lines.

Beardies with those colors, or morphs, as they are known, could not survive in the wild.

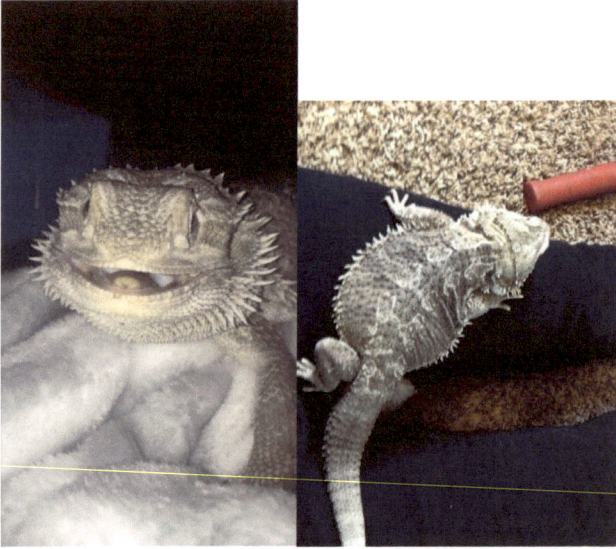

Above, a "normal" Beardie. Below, a special morph

Chapter Three
Are Males or Females Better Pets?

Both males and females make great pets, but there are specific things to watch for with each. Female Bearded Dragons, just like chickens, can lay eggs even if they are never near a male. Not all will, but you need to be ready just in case. If your female starts digging in her cage, she may be trying to lay eggs. You need to provide her with a "lay box" where she can dig and tunnel to lay her eggs. When she's finished, you need to dig out the eggs and freeze them before discarding. Producing and laying eggs is stressful for both the females and their owners, but you won't know in advance whether or not yours will.

Choosing a male Beardie eliminates the worry about eggs, but you have additional issues with hormones. Males, especially young "teenage" ones, can get quite testy during breeding season even if they are solitary pets. The hormone driven behavior changes don't happen with all males, but you need to be alert. Somehow they know when it's breeding season, even if no other Bearded Dragons are around. It's vital that you spend time and work with them every day to keep their behavior in check during breeding season.

Having a good Bearded Dragon for a pet boils down to temperment, which is not determined by gender. The way they're raised makes all the difference; however, there are temperment differences with some of the different "morphs" or colors. Reds, males in particular, are more aggressive from birth and even more so during breeding season. Lots of attention and care is necessary to keep them tamed down.

Newly hatched red baby, ready to bite.

Chapter Four
If my female lays eggs, should I go ahead and breed her?

Absolutely not, unless you want to embark on a huge amount of work and lots of expense. Breeding also puts your female at risk, since sex between Beardies is rough. Males often bite, so your girl may have wounds on her head and back. Laying materials, such as incubators, hatching materials, special feeding regimen for newborns—are all necessary after a successful breeding.

If you're thinking that raising Beardies would be a great way to make money, think again. There is already an oversupply of normals—that is, plain colored Bearded Dragons with no special genetics—needing suitable homes. Raising special morphs can be more profitable, but purchasing good breeding stock, understanding Beardie genetics, collecting all the needed materials for breeding, and feeding voracious babies for three to five months before selling them, can

14

cost a small fortune with no guarantee of profits.

If your Beardie female lays eggs, freeze them and throw them out.

Incubated babies hatching in containers.

Chapter Five
Are Babies or Adults Better for My First Bearded Dragon?

A friendly adult Bearded Dragon is probably the best for first-time Beardie owners. The best sources for finding one are rescue organizations or local animal shelters, since they will usually be able to provide information on the Beardie's health and temperament. You can also often find one through neighborhood internet groups or market places, but you're more likely to be dealing with people looking to re-home their animals. You may find a wonderful one that way, but might also find one with health or temperament issues—perhaps even the reason the owner is trying to find a new home.

Temperament is easy to check. The Beardie should not be afraid of someone approaching the cage. The owner should be able to remove it from the cage easily, and hold it without the Beardie trying to bite.

Health is trickier to assess. The fat pads on the head should be plump, not sunken in.

The body should be well filled out, rather than wrinkled, since wrinkled skin can be an indication of dehydration. You should not be able to see the bones of the spine or ribs. Both eyes should be clear, and the skin should be clean and free of sore spots or injuries. The stance should be normal, with no bowed legs, and the gait should be even and properly upright on all four legs. A healthy animal won't shake or startle. If there is fecal material in the cage, it should be well-formed, not runny.

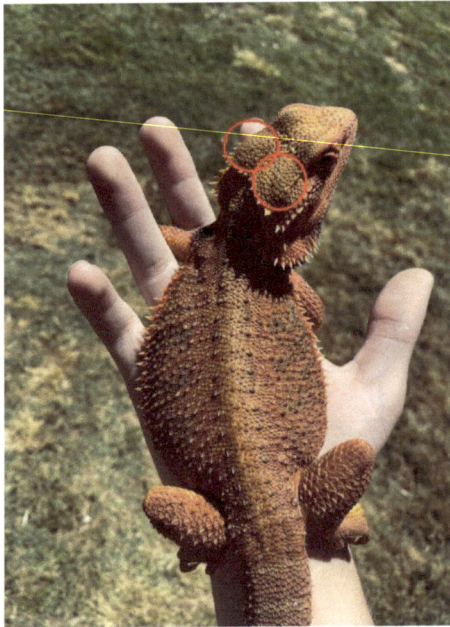

Red circles mark plump fat pads on healthy adult

Chapter Six
If I Get a Baby Bearded Dragon, How Old Should It Be?

Getting a baby Beardie is exciting, but you want to be sure the animal you get is old enough and healthy enough to thrive in a new home. To make that happen, you need to look both at age and weight. The age should be about three months, with a minimum weight of 25 to 30 grams.

We don't recommend shopping for a baby Beardie at a large chain pet store, since they often sell babies that are too young and/or too small for optimum health. There are pet stores that specialize in reptiles that should be a better choice.

If you are purchasing a baby Beardie on the internet, do your homework and ask lots of questions, including the age and weight. Also, investigate the seller, too. Have they been in business long? Do they have testimonials from happy customers? Were they willing to talk to you and answer all your questions? If you aren't comfortable with them, their animal might not be the best choice for you.

Babies above are healthy, but too small for adoption. The ones below are ready for new homes.

Chapter Seven
Are Bearded Dragons Hard To Care For?

Beardie care is not difficult, once you understand and master the basics—proper size cage, good nutrition, required UVB light exposure, proper temperature, and health monitoring—your pet should be just fine.

Make sure you get your advice from Bearded Dragon experts, not someone with only a smattering of knowledge, or someone who is focused on selling you products. Remember that all the care components mentioned above cannot substitute for proper socialization or overcome poor health in the pet you chose.

Two Reds, relaxing in their cages

Chapter Eight
What is the best type of cage for a Bearded Dragon?

The most important feature for a Beardie cage is size—it must have adequate room for an adult, which can reach up to 24 inches from its nose to the tip of its tail. If you already have a small enclosure available for a young one, that's fine, but be aware that you will need to move to a bigger cage fairly soon. If you are purchasing a cage for your first Beardie, get the biggest one you can. You also need good ventilation, and room for both a long UVB fixture and a heat emitter. Cages that open from the top can be scary, especially for young ones, because the motion of a hand coming down can trigger their instinctual fear of predators, like birds.

There are several different types of cages available, all with advantages and drawbacks. Here are the most common types to choose from:

Glass cages give good visibility, but tend to lose heat easier than other types. You need to pay very close attention to the temperature since it may vary more than you realize. You also must be careful about cracks or chips in the surface. Melamine cages do a much better job of holding heat than glass, and can be easier to keep clean than glass. They have sliding glass doors in front for good visibility and easy cleaning. You need to watch the caulking seals between the walls and bottom, since if it pulls away, water can get into the pressed wood and cause it to swell.

PVC (Plastic) cages are much lighter than Melamine and have better ventilation. The doors can be either glass or plexiglass, and can slide side to side like the melamine cages, or hinge to open from either the top or bottom. They are very easy to clean, but are also much more expensive than the other types.

Don't forget that your Beardies need to spend time out of the cage with you. Make the cage the most perfect environment you can, but make sure they get to spend plenty of time outside of it to enjoy your company and explore.

Chapter Nine
What Is The Best Material For The Bottom Of Tthe Bearded Dragon's Cage?

Cleanliness and safety are the most important things to consider for the bottom of the Beardie's cage. Just like the different types of cages, the various kinds of substrate all have advantages and disadvantages:

<u>Tile squares</u> are great for easy cleaning and to wear down the Beardie's claws. It does not, however, give them any traction for moving around. The only downside is installation—you must not use adhesives because the fumes aren't safe. You must also be sure to completely seal between tiles to prevent water and insects from getting underneath.

<u>Reptile Carpets</u> look good in a cage and provide a nice surface for Beardies to move around on; however, their claws can get stuck in the threads. Reptile Carpets are impractical for people with multiple Beardies, since they must be removed, washed and dried (never in the washer or dryer), so you need to

have at least one in reserve for each cage. They are designed to be washed and dried once a week, but that means a lot of fecal material will collect, which can create both odor problems and an unhygienic environment.

Loose substrate (sand or dirt) looks good and permits the Beardie to dig around, which they enjoy. If you feed your Beardie outside of the cage, the loose substrate can be a good choice for adults. If you own a young Bearded Dragon or feed inside the cage, loose substrate can be dangerous because of the danger of accidental ingestion and impaction. In other words, both youngsters and adults will eat pieces of the substrate with their food and have it collect in a mass in their intestinal tracts.

Paper isn't pretty, but it is the choice of breeders and people who own multiple reptiles because it makes the cages easy to keep clean with none of the disadvantages of tile, reptile carpet, or loose substrates. Fecal material is immediately visible, and cleaning is as simple as pulling out one sheet and replacing it with another. Never use paper towels because the babies, and some adults, will try to eat it, but newspaper, butcher paper, or paper used for moving all work well. The only disadvantage is that insects and worms can crawl beneath it and out of sight for the Beardie, but you'll see them when you remove the paper.

Chapter Ten
What is UVB and why is it important for Bearded Dragons?

UVB is the component of sunlight that keeps Beardies healthy and is necessary for digesting their food. They need 12 hours of UVB light per day, or ½ hour of natural sunlight. Since most Beardies don't spend their days running free in the yard, you must provide UVB through a lighting fixture for their cage.

If you have a cage with a screen top, your UVB fixture has to be on top of the cage, shining straight down. For other cages, the UVB fixture is attached inside the top of the cage. Don't use the round UVB bulbs such as the one in kits, since the UVB just goes down rather than filling the cage. Unless the Beardie hangs out directly below the bulb all the time, they won't receive an adequate amount. The long bulbs, either fluorescent or LED (which are much better), will provide UVB throughout the entire cage except for when the Beardie crawls under its hide.

Remember that the UVB properties of the bulbs only last a year, which means even if the bulb is lighting up, it must be replaced at least once a year to be effective. If you notice your Beardie throwing up after eating, or see that its food passes through its system without changing in appearance, that is an indication that it is not getting enough UVB.

Top is a glass cage with UVB and heat on top,
Bottom is Melamine cage with both inside at top

Chapter Eleven
How hot should the Bearded Dragon's cage be?

Each Beardie cage needs to have a range of temperatures, with both a cool side and a hot side. Heat lamps, or heat emitters, need to be either attached inside the cage on the hot end, or aimed down on top of cages with a screen top. The heat sources—lamps or emitters—send heat straight down to what is the hottest part of the cage, which should be no more than 105 degrees. Your Beardie will love basking under the heat source on a hide, rock, or hammock, as long as the heat there does not exceed the 105 degrees.

The cool side of the cage is just as important, and should not be lower than 80 degrees. The cool side is the best place for food dishes, especially salads.

Top, Dragon basking on top of hide.
Bottom, babies on top of frog

Chapter Twelve
What does a Bearded Dragon need in its cage?

Each Beardie should have a hide in its cage for privacy in the dark when it chooses. Hides come in various sizes and styles, but must be big enough for the Berdie to climb inside and turn around. Something for basking under the heat source is appreciated by Beardies, whether on the top of the hide, a special climbing branch, or a basking hammock. It needs to be positioned under the heat, but there should be sufficient space under the heat to not burn the Beardie.

Shallow food dishes are necessary if you feed inside the cage. Live foods and salads should never be placed on the bottom of the cage to prevent ingestion of the substrate and to keep the feeding more hygienic.

Water dishes are not necessary, in fact, they can send the humidity level too high and cause respiratory issues. Beardies don't like to drink standing water, in fact, they're more likely to poop in it than to drink it. Bearded

Dragons get their hydration from the water in their salads, frequent misting, and periodic bathing outside of the cage.

Female digging holes to lay her eggs,
definitely in need of a bath!

Chapter Thirteen
What do Bearded Dragons eat?

Beardies eat both live food and salads. Babies need 80% live food and 20% salads, but the percentages are reversed for adults. Live food means a variety of different worms, Dubia and red roaches, crickets, and blackfly larvae. Just like with cage bottom materials, there are pros and cons for different foods:

<u>Worms</u> include lots of varieties, and various things to consider for each type. Affordability varies between the types of worms, and some are much harder to keep until they fed to the Beardies. All worms should be gut-loaded prior to being fed to the Beardies. That just means they should have been fed very high nutrient food before they become food. Some are gut-loaded prior to shipment to owners, so checking on the vendor is a good idea. Worms should be dusted with nutrients prior to feeding to the Beardies to make sure they are getting the proper amount of calcium and other nutrients they need.

Superworms are a great staple for adult and juvenile Beardies, but are too large for babies or some small juveniles to eat.
Mealworms are nutritious staples for adults, but the shells are too hard for babies to eat.
Phoenix Worms come in different sizes, and are perfect for babies from newborn on up. They are also known as blackfly larvae, or calcium worms.
Waxworms are an excellent treat for Beardies, but are too high in fat to feed as a staple.
Hornworms are excellent for high protein and low fat, but are very expensive. They are also more difficult to keep before feeding.
Butterworms are great supplements for their high protein, low fat, and considerable calcium, but are even more expensive than Hornworms.
Silkworms are the highest in nutrients, and can be fed to Beardies of all ages. You may have to purchase them as tiny hatchlings and raise them.
Roaches are excellent, nutritious foods for Beardies. The two kinds of roach feeders are Dubia and Red Runner. Neither can infest your house like cockroaches, since they are

bred for feeders. Baby Bearded Dragons, juveniles, and adults all love roaches, but must be fed the appropriate sizes.

Crickets are the most common food stocked by pet stores for Beardies, and fed by pet owners. Since they are available in multiple sizes, from pinheads for newborns to full-grown crickets for adult reptiles, they can be given to all ages. There are two potential problems to be aware of if you feed with crickets. First of all, you should not leave live crickets in the cage to hang out until the Beardie gets hungry. They can bite the Beardies, and often target the eyes and mouth. Secondly, crickets carry parasites that will thrive in the Bearded Dragons bodies. Owners who feed crickets should always get a fecal examination done at least once a year so they can treat as needed.

Salads are essential for Beardie good health, but some turn their noses up at the greens and wait for something that moves. You can try is removing any bugs in the cage prior to offering the salad. If it's their only choice, they're likely to eat it. Even better, you can teach your Beardie to love salads. Adding things like small amounts of bee pollen, fruit, superfoods (Repashy in multiple flavors, such as pumpkin), or organic baby food will add eye appeal to draw the Beardie to the salad, and sweet flavor to satisfy their taste buds.

Once they discover that salads can taste delicious, they're much more likely to dive in. Some vegetables and fruits are nutritious, while others are not. Still others can be harmful. Always check a reliable source before adding a new vegetable or fruit to your Bearded Dragon's salad. You also need to be careful about the amount of sugar in salads, and only give fruit once in awhile because it can give Beardies mouth rot.

See the chart below for information on vegetable and fruits that are safe for your Bearded Dragon to eat:

Vegetable Staples:

Arugula	Bok choy	Cactus pads
Collard greens		Endive
Escarole		
Kale (a recent study revealed that it is okay after all)		
Mustard greens		Oak choy
Swiss chard		Turnip greens

Vegetables okay to feed sometimes:

Artichoke heart	Basil
Bell pepper	Carnation
Cilantro	Carrot greens
Cucumber, peeled	
Carrot, grated raw	Mint leaves
Clover (pesticide and herbicide free)	
Parsley	Rose petals

Squash, raw
Yam, grated raw

Vegetable **POISON**—do **NOT** feed to
your Bearded Dragon!
Avocado   Onion

Fruit Staples:
Cactus fruit (prickly pear)

Fruit okay to feed sometimes:
| Apples | Berries | Figs |
| Grapes | Melon | Peaches |

Fruit **POISON**—do **NOT** feed to
your Bearded Dragon!
Citrus   Rhubarb

Dry Bearded Dragon food is available at
large chain stores, where they are often touted
as complete foods that Beardies should have
every day. Live foods and fresh salads are far
better for your pet. In fact, many Beardies will
not eat it all if they are used to fresh food. It is
a good idea to have some on hand, however,
just in case of an emergency.

Red Beardie, first as a baby on the left,
then as an intensely colored juvenile on the right.

Chapter Fourteen
Can I have two Bearded Dragons together?

No, Bearded Dragons are solitary animals, and each one should have their own cage. Babies from the same clutch of eggs are usually kept together at first because they are the same size, but then are separated into much smaller groups to prevent nips and bites. When there is a substantial size difference between two Beardies in the same cage, the larger may try to eat the other one. Sometimes people will see a Beardie laying on top of another and think they are cuddling— they're not, it is dominance with the one on top keeping the one on the bottom from getting enough UVB.

If you put a male and female Beardie together in the same cage, the male may over-breed her. And Bearded Dragons aren't gentle with one another, so the female can end up with serious bites from the male. If you put two males together, they will fight to the death. Two females are sometimes okay together, even for an extended time, then turn on one another and fight with no warning. It is always better to house your Beardies in separate cages.

Male spotted another male outside of his cage, now is ready to attack and fight to the death.

Chapter Fifteen
Do Bearded Dragons need water?

Bearded Dragons originated in a desert environment, so do not need standing water in their cages. In fact, standing water can make the cage humidity too high, causing mouth rot. Also, Beardies don't trust standing water—in the wild, standing water might be bad—so are more likely to poop in it than drink it. But they need to be well hydrated. There are different methods to make sure that happens.

Beardies love to be misted, just like a favorite indoor plant. Misting makes them feel good and provides water through their skins. Don't overdo it though, or you'll elevate the cage humidity too much.

Beardies should have baths for several reasons. They clean up the animal and remove food or fecal material from the skin, making them a lot more pleasant to hold. Baths help old shed to work itself off. They will often duck their heads under the water and drink, which is a great for hydration. They need to be supervised closely, since Beardies also like to poop in the water. You don't want them to drink or soak in polluted water, so you have to be ready to change the water when they mess in it. A Bearded Dragon's bath should have warm water in a tub deep enough that they can't climb out of, but shallow enough that they can hold their heads out of the water and keep all four feet on the bottom.

Bearded Dragons can be taught to drink from a narrow tipped bottle, such as a condiment bottle. This isn't instinctual for them, but you can offer something tasty to get them used to the process.

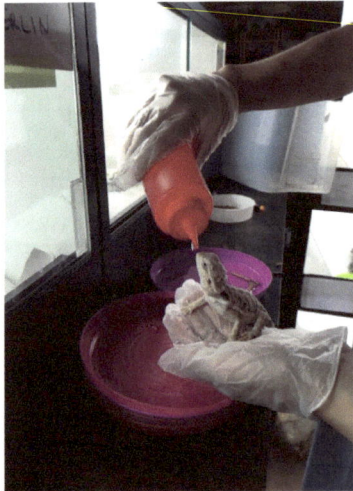

Young Beardie learning to drink from bottle

Chapter Sixteen
What health issues do Bearded Dragons have?

Bearded Dragons are generally healthy, hardy animals. The keys to keeping them that way are proper nutrition, adequate UVB, proper heat, and clean cages. You need to investigate any deviation from normal behavior, since it might indicate a health issue. Some of the most common health issues are as follows:

Parasites such as roundworms, tapeworms, hookworms, pinworms, giardia, and coccidiosis are common and will show up through a fecal test.

Metabolic bone disease (MBD) is the most common health problem, often in juveniles of less than two years old. This is generally caused by an improper diet or a lack of exposure to UVB.

<u>Infectious stomatitis (mouth rot)</u> is a bacterial infection of the gums and/or jaw bone.

<u>Respiratory infections, especially pneumonia</u>, can occur if Beardies are stressed, improperly fed, or in cages that are cold, dirty, or too humid.

<u>Adenovirus infection</u> is very common in young Beardies, but can hit older ones as well. They fail to thrive, are weak, often won't eat, and end up dying.

Chapter Seventeen

How can I find a vet that will treat a Bearded Dragon?

Vets that treat Beardies often have wording on their literature or websites about treating "exotic" animals. If you can't find one in your area, you still want to get routine fecal tests done to control parasites. Since Beardies are subject to many of the same parasites that infect cats and dogs, ask if the vet would just do a fecal test for you. Many of the medications are the same, and you can research dosages.

Navigator ("Normal" Beardie) checking out the GPS
display while out on a car ride.

Chapter Eighteen
Why Do Bearded Dragons Prices Vary So Much?

Pet stores usually sell what are called "normal" Bearded Dragons, often in the $30 to $50 range. The normals range from gray to brown, more similar to the ones that came from Australia long ago. Normals make great pets, so don't ignore them just because they're more common. The most important features of any Beardie are good health and temperament.

The Beardies advertised for hundreds or thousands of dollars are special "morphs," which is a word that refers to their genetics. These special morphs come in several colors, such as bright yellows, reds, brilliant orange, or pale gray. The patterns, such as blue bars or unusual stripes, can also add to the values. Some of the special morphs have personality traits or health issues associated with the colors, so it's important to do your homework before buying.

The different morphs also refer to the spiny scales. Normal Bearded Dragons are spiny all over, with extra long spines on the sides. Leatherbacks Beardies are smooth on their backs, but still have spines on their sides. And then there are Silkback (Silkie) Beardies. WARNING: Do not choose a Silkie for your first Beardie! While the smooth skin is appealing and the colors are vivid, they come with significant health issues. Their lifespans are much shorter. Shedding, which should be a simple process, is difficult and painful for Silkies, much like suffering a horrible sunburn every single month would be for a person.

The personalities of these special morphs are the same as normals, so spending much higher amounts to purchase one is a personal choice. Good health is far more important than a pretty color.

Chapter Nineteen
Is shedding a problem for Bearded Dragons?

Bearded Dragons shed skin from their entire bodies on a regular basis, about once a month. You can tell when they're getting ready when their colors look faded, because the old skin is getting ready to slough off. They may get a little testy just before shedding because it's uncomfortable. You can help lift off skin that is loose sticking up, but do not pull old skin off if it isn't already loose. Doing so would be very painful, much like pulling skin off a painful sunburn that hasn't yet begun to peel. Most Beardies handle the shedding process by themselves with no problems, but you can sometimes help if old skin is stuck, especially on their toes. The best way to help is to give them a bath, and brush the old skin off with a toothbrush.

Citrus Beardie partially covered in shed. Bright colored head and legs show new skin after shed removed.

Chapter Twenty
Unique Beardie Behaviors

Bearded Dragons have unique behaviors that are fun to watch, but sometimes difficult to understand.

Arm Waving is cute as can be—one leg raised, slowly circled around, then sometimes switched to the other leg. Waving behavior happens for three primary reasons. First, they're letting you know that they see you. Kind of like saying, I know you're there, so don't try to sneak up on me. Arm waving is also a submissive behavior, like a dog rolling over to show its belly. Arm waving can also be a mating behavior, sort of a cute, flirty behavior of saying they're interested.

Head Bobbing is more common for males, but females do it too. Dominance, stress, or mating are the primary reasons for head bobbing. Head bobbing will decrease as the Beardie gets used to a new environment, but may pop back during mating season.

Beard Puffing is what gives Bearded Dragons their name, and is very impressive to see. The beard puffs way out and turn black, making them look scary—and intimidation is what they're going for. Beard puffing can be for aggression, fear, discomfort, or an eagerness to mate, but as long as they are still exhibiting healthy behavior, there's nothing to worry about.

No wonder Bearded Dragons are such popular pets. They're fun to watch and seem to like the company of their human family members. Caring for them is relatively easy once you master the basic requirements. So, choose one with care, socialize it well, and enjoy your special pet for many years to come.

Male with black beard

About the Authors

This book is a family affair. The authors—Sheryl, Christopher, and Nicholas Wilson—are a mother and twin sons. When they rescued one Bearded Dragon, it turned into a love affair.

Then they rescued another, and another. The third, Toad, turned out to be full of eggs, which required the purchase of an incubator and all the materials needed to care for newborn Beardies. Their fascination grew over time, until they became breeders and founded Trilogy Dragons.

They are still enchanted with Bearded Dragons and love spending time with all of their animals.

All of the pictures are of Bearded Dragons owned by the authors. No matter how many they have, all are loved and handled often from birth.

You can find out more about the authors at their website, https://www.trilogydragons.com, or email them at trilogydragons@gmail.com.

Baby Beardies are so cute, but need to be handled.

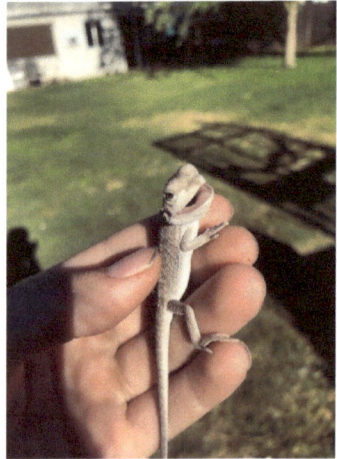

Glossary and Index

Bee pollen, Pg 33
   Bee pollen is a ball or pellet of field-
   gathered flower pollen packed by worker
   honeybees.

Black fly larvae, Pgs 31, 32
   Black soldier fly larvae, also known as
   phoenix worms and calcium worms.

Breed, Pgs 11, 13, 24, 37
   Mate and then produce offspring

Cage, Pgs 7, 8, 11, 15, 16, 19, 32, 33, 34, 34,
   35, 37, 29, 30, 31, 33, 37, 38, 39, 41, 42
   Enclosure that houses the Bearded
   Dragon

Calcium, Pgs 31, 32
   One of the alkaline earth metals, essential
   for bones and teeth

Captive bred, Pg 9
   Animals born in captivity

Clutch, Pg 37
   Eggs laid at one time, and the Bearded
   Dragon babies hatched from those eggs.

Cricket, Pgs 31, 33
   Insect used as reptile feeders

Dominance, Pgs 37, 49
   One exercising power over another

Dubia, Pgs 31, 32
   A type of roach raised for reptile feeders

Egg, Pgs 11, 13, 14, 37, 51
   An oval object which, when fertilized,
   contains a developing embryo

Environment, Pgs 9, 22, 24, 39, 49
   The surroundings in which an animal
   lives

Fecal (Poop), Pgs 16, 24, 33, 39, 40, 41, 43
   Relating to solid body waste

Fight, Pgs 37, 38
   Battle with one another

Genetic, Pgs 9, 13, 45
   Relating to genes or heredity

Gut-load, Pg 31
   Feeding a worm or insect high-quality
   food just before it is fed to a reptile

Hatch, Pgs 13, 32
   When the reptile emerges from its egg

Head bobbing, Pg 49
    When the head moves up and down

Health, Pgs 9, 15, 17, 19, 25, 33, 41, 45, 46,
    50
    State of mental or physical condition

Heat, Pgs 21, 22, 27, 29, 41
    High temperature

Hide, Pgs 25, 27, 29
    A shelter

Hormones, Pg 11
    Substance produced in an organism that
    regulates and stimulates specific cells or
    tissues into action

Hornworm, Pg 32
    The caterpillar of a hawk moth

Humidity, Pgs 29, 39
    The amount of moisture in the air

Hydrate, Pg 39
    Cause to absorb water

Impaction, Pg 24
    Intestines tightly filled with fecal material

Refers to Bearded Dragons with special genetics

Mouth rot, Pgs 34, 39, 42
Infection of the mouth and gum

Newborn, Pgs 13, 32, 33, 51
Newly hatched baby

Normal, Pgs 9, 13, 16, 41, 45, 46
Bearded dragons that resemble the ones originally from Australia

Nutrient, Pgs 31, 32
A substance that provides nourishment

Nutrition, Pgs 9, 19, 41
Providing food necessary for health and growth

Parasite, Pgs 33, 41, 43
An organism that lives inside a host animal

Pet allergies, Pg 7
A damaging immune response to pets

Phoenix worms, Pg 32
Also known as Black Fly Larvae or Calcium worms

Pinhead, Pg 33

Refers to smallest size of Phoenix worms
or crickets

Pneumonia, Pg 42
Bacterial or viral lung infection

Red runner, Pg 32
A special type of feeder roach

Repashy, Pg 33
A type of superfood that comes in several
flavors

Reptile Carpet, Pgs 23, 24
A special type of flooring for the bottom
of the reptile cage

Respiratory, Pgs 29, 42
Relating to respiration (breathing)

Roach, Pgs 31, 32, 33
Insects that are used as feeders

Salad, 27, 29, 30, 31, 33, 34, 35
A cold dish of various raw vegetables and
fruits

Shed, Pgs 39, 46, 47
The outer layer of skin comes off, to be
replaced by another one that has grown
underneath.

Personality as it affects behavior

Two beautiful Trilogy Dragon babies,
Citrus and Red on top, Zero on bottom

Bentley, below, thinks Liberty, above, is beautiful!

www.ingramcontent.com/pod-product-compliance
Lightning Source LLC
Chambersburg PA
CBHW041357090426
42739CB00005B/54